HOW THEY LIVED

A PIONEER WOMAN

THEODORE KNIGHT

Illustrated by
James Spence

ROURKE BOOK COMPANY, INC.
Vero Beach, Florida 32964

A Blackbirch Graphics Book.

Printed in the United States of America.

Library of Congress Cataloging-in-Publication Data

Knight, Theodore, 1946–
    A pioneer woman / by Theodore Knight; illustrated by James
Spence.
        p.   cm. — (How they lived)
    Includes index.
    ISBN 1-55916-038-1
    1. Women pioneers—West (U.S.)—Juvenile literature. 2. Frontier
and pioneer life—West (U.S.)—Juvenile literature. 3. West (U.S.)—
Social life and customs—Juvenile literature. [1. Frontier and pioneer
life—West (U.S.) 2. Pioneers. 3. Women—Biography.] I. Title. II.
Series: How they lived (Vero Beach, Fla.)
F596.K6   1994
978'.0082—dc20   94-741
                                                    CIP
Printed in the USA   AC

CONTENTS

ALL IN A DAY'S WORK

The cabin she and her husband built in the deep forest had a dirt floor and was only fourteen feet square. They lived in Oregon, on the western frontier. Men and women alike faced many hardships and dangers on the frontier.

Each morning, a pioneer woman would wake before the sun rose. She would cook breakfast for her husband and children over a fire. Next, she might feed and milk the family's cows. In the summer, a pioneer woman would plant and tend a large vegetable garden. This was one of her most important tasks. A family depended on the vegetables from their garden both to eat during the summer season, and to store for supplies during

A pioneer's fireplace was used both to cook food and heat the home.

A pioneer woman cared for her family's garden.

the winter. A pioneer family either raised or hunted almost everything they ate.

During the day, a pioneer woman had many other responsibilities. She had to wash and mend clothes and bake for her family. She cooked the three meals of the day in a fireplace. She made all of her family's clothes— even their shoes. Cheese and butter were made from cows' milk. The light in a family's

cabin came from candles that were made by hand. These candles usually burned very quickly. If the candle supply got low, a pioneer woman had to work all day in order to make more.

The work day for a pioneer woman usually lasted about sixteen hours. Then she would be able to climb into bed to rest and regain her energy for the hard work that awaited her the next day.

THE AMERICAN FRONTIER

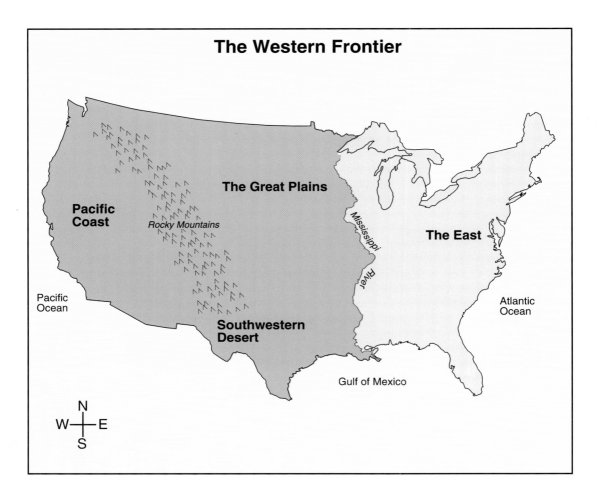

The first white people who traveled west of the Mississippi River were explorers and fur trappers. Soon, they were followed by pioneer men and women who wanted to build homes and settle down in the undeveloped West.

The western frontier was really made up of three large regions. Between the Mississippi River and the Rocky Mountains, the land was very flat. The northern and eastern part of this flat land consisted of wide, grassy plains. Today, that part of the United States is known as the Great Plains. To the south and west of this region, the land was extremely dry. This area was known as the Southwestern Desert. On the other side of the Rocky Mountains, was the Pacific Coast region. This was a land of mountains, forests, and deep green valleys that stretched all the way to the Pacific Ocean.

The pioneers who settled in the western lands struggled with many different challenges and hardships. On the flat plains, they had to work hard to break the thick sod in order to plant their crops. They suffered from the wind and sun in the summer, and the wind and snow in the winter. In the dry desert lands, the pioneers fought dust storms and intense heat and it was difficult to find enough water to keep their cattle alive. On the Pacific Coast, there was often a lot of rain and dampness. The pioneers there were faced with clearing away dense forests of huge trees and thick brush before they could build their homes and begin to farm.

Pioneers often used oxen to help with the difficult work of clearing and plowing the land.

How They Traveled

Pioneer families traveled slowly across the frontier in wagon trains.

Most pioneer families traveled west by wagon, in groups called wagon trains. Many of these groups set out on their journeys in the early spring. Before the next winter, the wagons needed to have traveled 2,000 miles. If they didn't move quickly enough, the Rocky Mountains would be blocked with winter snow. Travelers would then be stuck between the mountains and the desert without enough supplies to last until spring.

The wagons most families traveled in had wooden bodies that were about ten feet long and four feet wide. A canvas, stretched over wooden strips, made a curved cover over the wagon. Most of the wagons were pulled by oxen. The oxen were better suited to the long, difficult trip than horses. Everything a pioneer family needed for months on the trail was packed in their wagon.

Life along the wagon trail was very hard. The pioneers walked all day long in a thick cloud of dust raised by the animals and wagons. There was little time to stop. It was necessary to travel as many miles as possible every day.

Many people died during these long trips. Some people died from accidents, but many died from illness. A terrible disease, called cholera, killed many travelers. In 1850, a doctor who traveled to Oregon reported that up to 3,000 people had died of cholera on the wagon trail that year.

WHO THEY WERE

Many pioneer women were married and had children. Often, they were the wives of eastern farmers whose land was either worn out or too small. These pioneers dreamed of having large pieces of unsettled western land on which to plant their crops and build their homes. After the end of the American Civil War, in 1865, many soldiers whose businesses or farms had been destroyed during the war set out to the frontier to get a fresh start.

Some pioneer women were the wives of city dwellers. Their husbands wanted to head west because they believed that greater opportunities for success and independence awaited them there. These women were less prepared than the farmers' wives were for the hard life they found along the trail and on the frontier.

There were also pioneer women traveling west who were either missionaries, or wives of missionaries. Although they planned to make their homes on the frontier, they were not seeking land, independence, or success. Some of these missionaries planned to teach the Christian religion to the Native American tribes that lived on the frontier.

In addition, a fairly large number of pioneers were immigrant families who came from different parts of Europe. They ventured into the frontier when they learned that the land in the American West was practically free for anyone who wanted to claim it.

Not all of the pioneer women were wives and mothers. Single women also went west. On the frontier, women had more freedom and independence than they did in the East. There was a huge amount of work to be done, and women on the frontier who did their share of the work were treated as the equals of men.

Opposite: A pioneer family gathered wood together and transported it in a hand-made wheelbarrow.

WHY THEY WENT WEST

The availability of inexpensive land encouraged people to make the long, difficult journey to settle the western frontier. The U.S. government offered this land to anyone who wanted to settle on it. However, settlers were required to clear the land and put up a cabin within six months. If they remained on their claim for seven years, the land then became legally

The first settlers of America struggled to clear and build on their new land.

A frontier family traveled across the prairie to reach their home.

theirs. In some parts of the frontier, a single claim was 160 acres. In other areas, claims were as large as 640 acres.

Federal law allowed single women to claim land. It also allowed women to hold the title to (legally own) land if their husbands died. For these reasons, many single women traveled to the West seeking opportunities they did not have in the East.

Many of the women who went west had worked in factories in New England. There, they were paid barely enough money to survive. They often worked from before dawn until after dusk in miserable, dirty conditions. For these "factory girls," fresh air, sunshine, and a chance to build a better life made both the hardships and danger of frontier travel and settlement worth the risk.

Before the Civil War ended, another group of men and women also moved west—slaves and ex-slaves. Slavery was against the law in the western territories of the United States, so freed or escaped slaves headed for the frontier. There, they knew they were safe from being sent back into slavery.

BUILDING A HOME

Once a pioneer family found a good place to settle, they could not spare much time to build a home. Land had to be cleared and crops planted in order to have food for the next winter.

Many pioneer families lived in tents, or small open shelters, while they built their homes. Often, these shelters had only three sides. A large fire was kept burning at all times in front of the open side.

A pioneer family had to build a home from whatever materials the region provided. Men and women worked alongside each other. In forested areas, most pioneers built log cabins, using the many trees that they had chopped down in order to clear the land.

Temporary shelters such as these housed pioneer families while they built permanent homes.

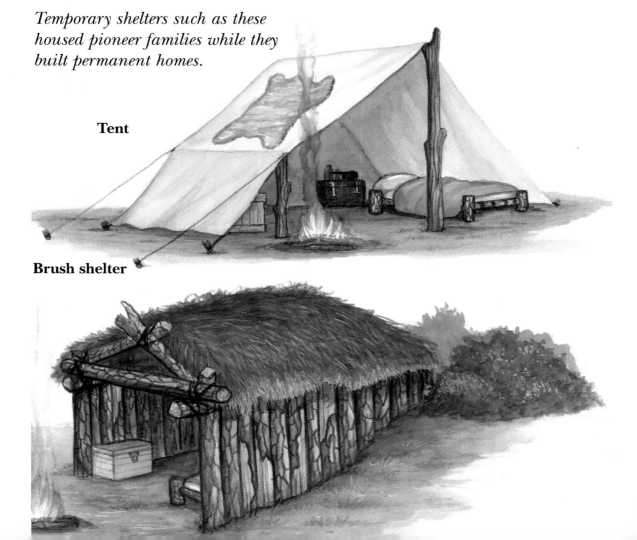

Tent

Brush shelter

On the prairies, people built sod houses. Sod is soil in which dirt and grass roots are tightly packed together. The sod on the prairies was several feet thick. Sod huts were made by slicing this hard soil into blocks and using them like bricks to build walls. Roofs were made

Pioneer homes were made of wood in the forested regions of the frontier, and of sod in the prairies.

of canvas, or more sod that was supported by branches woven together. Sod huts were warm and snug during the winter. However, they were also very dark and dirty.

No matter what kind of home a pioneer family built, it shared one feature. It was very small. Entire families lived in cabins and huts that were only eight or ten feet long and eight or ten feet wide.

Sod house

Log cabin

A Hard Life

Pioneer women needed to be both brave and resourceful on the frontier. They had to provide whatever medical care they or their families needed, as any doctor was usually hours—or even days—away over rough trails. Any illness or injury could turn into a deadly problem.

Pioneer women made most of their own medicines from household ingredients, alcohol, wild plants, and roots. Women also had to deliver their own babies, although they sometimes had the help of a family member or another settler's wife.

Whether they lived in log cabins or sod huts, pioneer women found that conditions were little better than they had been on the wagon trail. The floors of their new homes were usually made of dirt. In sod huts, dirt fell steadily down from the roof and walls. Water dripped in during every rain storm, and most roofs leaked badly. There were no glass windows and, in the summer, insects could fly in and out of the house. In the winter, snow and cold winds penetrated through every crack and hole. Under these conditions, pioneer women had trouble keeping clothes, bedding, and their families clean, warm, and dry.

Few settlers had much furniture. Families were lucky if they had managed to bring a bed or a couple of chairs with them along the wagon trail. Most cabins were furnished with a rough table and some benches, all made from split logs. Food, clothing, tools, and any other supplies a frontier family had were stored in boxes or baskets that were left over from the wagon trip west.

Opposite: Pioneer families lived in sparsely furnished homes and ate whatever they could grow, gather, or hunt.

16

A Pioneer Woman's Tools

Few pioneer women were able to take their heavy metal cook stoves with them to the frontier. Meals were cooked on a fire outside of a family's shelter, or in a rough stone or clay fireplace inside a cabin or sod hut. Most of the cooking was done in large, heavy iron pots that hung over the fire on a metal hook called a crane. Meat was roasted on a metal spit. Baking was done inside a covered iron kettle set on the hearth close to the fire.

A pioneer woman made nearly everything her family wore. She would spin cotton, wool, or flax on a spinning wheel to make yarn. She would weave the yarn into cloth on a loom. Then, she would cut the cloth and sew the clothes. If she could get cattle or buffalo hides, she would turn these into leather and make outer clothing and shoes.

A pioneer woman didn't have many cleaning tools. A simple broom made with corn husks or twigs was used to sweep the floor. She would make the soap used for laundry

Opposite: Frontier women prepared meals over outdoor fires.

and bathing by boiling animal fat and ashes together.

A pioneer woman also had to be familiar with the tools men used. She could handle an axe, a hoe, a hammer, and a gun. She could harness and drive oxen and horses. Her labor was very important in helping the family's claim prosper. A pioneer woman had to be self-sufficient and prepared, as she never knew when an illness, an injury, or even a death might leave her to carry on all the work by herself.

Spinning wheels (front) and weaving looms (in the background) were essential tools for pioneer women.

GROWING, HUNTING, AND GATHERING FOOD

Often, pioneers did not have a wide variety of foods to eat. Vegetables like corn, beans, peas, squash, potatoes, carrots, and turnips were popular because all of these things could be safely stored for long periods of time. The pioneers always tried to have as much food stored as possible. They could never tell when a crop might fail or wild game might become hard to find.

Corn was frequently dried and then ground up into rough corn flour. The flour would either be used in baking, or mixed with hot water to make corn mush. Dried beans and peas would last unspoiled for a long time. Squash, potatoes, turnips, and carrots all stayed fresh for months if stored in a cool, dry place.

Most of the meat that the pioneers ate came from wild animals. Although many settlers had cows, sheep, and chickens, they depended on these animals for their milk, wool, and eggs. They would butcher their own animals only if one became too old or sick to produce.

There were few stores. There was milk to drink only if a family owned a cow. Otherwise, there was only water or coffee. The pioneers had to either buy their coffee or make a substitute. Pioneer women relied on their imaginations to create good coffee replacements. Some women ground up dried peas or corn and added small amounts of roots or tree bark for flavor. Ground acorns were a popular substitute for coffee.

Sugar was also scarce on the frontier. Pioneer women used honey and molasses to sweeten food and drinks. In the summer, lucky pioneer families might have been able to find wild fruits or berries to add variety to their meals.

Opposite: Pioneers had to hunt deer and other animals in order to have any meat to eat.

20

RAISING AND CARING FOR A FAMILY

A frontier woman had to know how to dress a wound.

The size of a pioneer family was always important. The family had to build its own shelter and provide almost all of its own food. It was dangerous for everyone if there were more people than there was food to go around. Also, there was a limit as to how many people could live in a tiny cabin or hut. However, as a child grew older, he or she could help with the work that needed to be done.

Death was a very common occurrence on the frontier. Mothers and infants often died in childbirth. Adults and children frequently became ill and died. A pioneer woman had to be able to act as both nurse and doctor for her family, as well as for herself.

Diseases like cholera, smallpox, and malaria were often causes of death during this time. No one really understood how germs were spread. It was not unusual for several members of the same family to become sick and die at nearly the same time. Some diseases were very contagious and killed quickly. A person could become sick and die from cholera overnight.

Because sanitary conditions were not good, food poisoning was another common problem on the frontier. There were also wounds and injuries—related to all of the hard work being done—that required treatment. Trees fell on people, axes and knives slipped, cattle and horses trampled their owners, and guns went off by accident. Without nearby doctors and hospitals, pioneer women did the best they could to help their families. Often, there was little that could be done for badly broken bones, deep wounds, and internal injuries. Whenever a pioneer woman faced a serious disease or injury, all she could do was to try and make the patient comfortable.

Many pioneer women often hunted in order to feed their families.

FRONTIER ENTERTAINMENT

A pioneer woman's life was not all hardship and sadness. People worked extremely hard on the frontier, but they also made an effort to have fun.

Most pioneer homes only contained a few books, but people read them over and over again. Often, they read aloud to one another. Since reading material was scarce, pioneers read anything they could get their hands on. They read almanacs, mail-order catalogs, months-old newspapers, and letters—anything that had words on it. Books were prized.

It was not unusual for frontier families to travel more than forty miles by horseback, or in a wagon, to attend a party or dance with other pioneer families. Some people had instruments—fiddles, guitars, accordions, banjos, or harmonicas—and provided the music needed for dancing. Often, when distances were great or the weather was bad, these gatherings lasted all night. People would enjoy a big meal, then dance, play games, and talk until dawn. In the morning,

Opposite: Settlers on the frontier found time to enjoy themselves.

they would eat a big breakfast before setting out for home.

Quilting bees were a popular form of entertainment for women on the frontier. A group of women would take turns gathering in one another's homes. At each house, they would all work together stitching a quilt for the hostess. During these get-togethers, women would keep up with what was going on in their community. These quilting bees also provided the pioneer women with a group setting in which to talk about how to solve a particular problem within the community.

Pioneer women had little time to themselves. However, a large number of them had one form of private entertainment. Many pioneer women kept detailed diaries. In their diaries, they not only described daily events, they also recorded many of their private thoughts. These diaries were preserved by children, grandchildren, and even great-grandchildren. Today, we know a great deal about daily life on the frontier—and about the hard life of pioneer women—because we can read their diaries.

RELIGION AND EDUCATION

Because of the isolated lives that most of the earliest settlers led, there were very few chances for families to attend church. For the same reason, few children ever went to school. As time passed and more people settled in an area, more churches and schools were built.

Until that time, a pioneer wife and mother was solely responsible for her family's religious activities and also provided whatever education her children received.

Religion in pioneer homes usually meant reading from the Bible and perhaps saying family prayers together. Education at home would have meant learning to read—often from the family's Bible—and learning to do simple arithmetic.

As settlements began to grow and travel became less difficult, pioneer families joined together in large groups at religious camp meetings. People would gather from great distances in a field or clearing in the forest to listen to preachers, sing hymns, and pray together. These camp meetings usually lasted several days. Families slept in tents, in their wagons, and under the stars. In the evenings, when the preaching, praying, and singing was over, people gathered around campfires and talked. Often, the annual camp meeting was the only chance pioneers had all year to meet anyone at all outside of a few of their closest neighbors.

People on the frontier often gathered for large church meetings.

INDEPENDENT PIONEER WOMEN

Not all pioneer women had families. Many women went to the West alone, or found themselves alone once they arrived there due to a tragedy along their journey.

The most common occupation for an independent woman on the frontier was teaching. When the frontier became settled enough for schools to be built, many jobs for teachers became available. The pay was very low and the conditions were often hard. However, for many young women in the East, teaching on the frontier was an improvement over the jobs they had as "factory girls." Frontier teachers were usually paid only a few dollars per month and the families of the students usually took turns providing a teacher with meals and a place to sleep.

Many women on the frontier also ran boardinghouses, did laundry, cooked, and baked. The cattle ranches of the Southwest, and the Rocky Mountain mining camps, were filled with men who were glad to pay to have a clean place to sleep or to have their clothes cleaned. Boardinghouse operators, cooks, and laundresses made large sums of money.

In general, independent pioneer women did everything that men did. Several women created an entire new agricultural industry. The very first grape and raisin growers in California were women. Also, many ranches in the Southwest were owned and operated by women. There were even female doctors and lawyers in the West, long before there were any back in the East.

Some women took pride in doing the toughest jobs available. A woman named Arizona Mary earned fame for the huge loads of freight that she hauled with her giant wagon. Charlie Pankhurst drove a stagecoach for twenty years. It was discovered she was a woman only when she died in 1879.

Pioneer women often took jobs as schoolteachers.

THE END OF THE FRONTIER

As more and more people moved west and settled, the frontier gradually disappeared. Houses made of lumber, shingles, and brick replaced the cabins and huts. Rough trails were replaced by wagon roads. The railroads arrived, making travel much faster and cheaper. The telegraph came, allowing people to communicate quickly with one another.

The end of the frontier meant the end of many of the hardships that the early women settlers faced. However, it did not mean the end of western women's pioneering spirit.

The western frontier had given women the chance to show that they could handle difficult situations. They had

The growth of railroads made travel much faster and easier on the frontier.

shown that they could meet challenges of hard work as well as men could. They had shown that they could own property and manage businesses. It was only fair, western women said, that they be given a voice in their government. They demanded the right to vote.

A national law giving women the right to vote was not passed until 1920. Most states that were east of the Mississippi River denied women that right. West of the Mississippi, however, women gained the right to vote much earlier. When Wyoming Territory gave women the right to vote in 1870, it was the only place in the world where they had that right. When Wyoming became a state in 1890, it refused to join the union unless women were allowed to keep the right to vote.

Pioneer women of the western frontier saw hardships as challenges to be overcome. Where others saw dangers, they saw new opportunities. Their courage and hard work are an important part of our nation's heritage.

GLOSSARY

almanac A yearly booklet giving weather forecasts, planting tips, tide charts, phases of the moon, and other useful information and advice.

cholera An infectious disease that is often fatal.

crane An iron rod with a hook on the end from which pots are hung over an open fire.

diary A personal, daily record of events and experiences.

flax A plant that has fibers that can be made into yarn.

hearth The brick or stone floor of a fireplace that extends in front of the fire itself.

heritage Traditions and beliefs passed from one generation to the next.

immigrant One who leaves one country in order to settle permanently in another.

loom A device for weaving thread or yarn together to make cloth.

malaria A disease causing chills, fever, and sweating, spread by mosquito bites.

molasses A thick sweet syrup made from various plants.

quilt A bed covering made by stitching together two sheets of cloth, or small patches of cloth, and putting fluffy cotton stuffing between them.

smallpox A deadly disease characterized by headaches, chills, backaches, fever, and skin blisters.

sod Soil that is held together by masses of roots.

spit An iron rod that is pushed through a piece of meat that is then suspended over an open fire.

INDEX

Acknowledgments and Photo Credits
Cover art by Gene Biggs. Interior artwork by James Spence. Pages 7, 12, 13,
19, 23, 30: North Wind Picture Archives.
Map by Blackbirch Graphics, Inc.